CRYSTAL CLEAR

tangerine press

an imprint of

SCHOLASTIC

www.scholastic.com

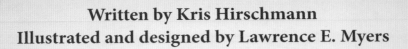

Written by Kris Hirschmann
Illustrated and designed by Lawrence E. Myers

Published by Tangerine Press, an imprint of Scholastic Inc., 557 Broadway; New York, NY 10012

Scholastic Canada Ltd.
Markham, Ontario

Scholastic Australia Pty. Ltd
Gosford NSW

Scholastic New Zealand Ltd.
Greenmount, Auckland

10 9 8 7 6 5 4 3 2 1

ISBN-10: 0-545-02113-8

ISBN-13: 978-0-545-02113-5

Made in China

Contents

LET'S GET ONE THING CRYSTAL CLEAR

Yes, this book will show you how to grow stuff. But you won't find any fruits or veggies between these covers. This book is all about growing **crystals**, which are more like rocks than food. (Mostly. There are exceptions, but we'll get to that later.) So don't expect to fill your belly as you work your way through this book. But do prepare to fill your mind with dazzling sights and fascinating facts. Read the notes on the next couple of pages. Then it's time to get growing!

WHAT EXACTLY IS A CRYSTAL, ANYWAY?

The quickie explanation: **Crystals** are solid substances in which the **atoms** and **molecules** form repeating patterns.

Whoa! Did you get that? No? Okay, look at it this way:

Imagine you're peering into the world's most powerful microscope. You can actually see a **crystal's** tiniest particles. Because of their properties, these particles form little squares, rectangles, or other shapes when they line up next to each other. Countless trillions of these shapes then join together to make larger shapes. When enough shapes join, they form **crystals** that you can see.

The joining-up process doesn't stop when a **crystal** becomes visible, of course. A **crystal** will get bigger and bigger as long as new particles stick to its sides. You guessed it—it's growing! And that process, friends, is what this book is all about.

By the way, what's up with those red words? Oh, right, they're vocabulary terms. Check the last page of this book for more info.

CRYSTAL'S TRIVIA CORNER

Hi there! My name is Crystal, and as you'll soon discover, I'm a sucker for trivia. Check out the fun facts I've pulled together for you throughout this book.

SPIKE'S SCIENCE SPOT

Spike's the name, and science is my game. I'll be giving you the inside scoop on the experiments in this book. Look for my blurb next to every experiment.

HERE'S WHAT YOU GET

This book comes with lots of stuff that will help you to grow the biggest, best crystals anywhere!

Crystal trees
It's a snap to grow fluffy trees with the tree cutouts, liquid packet, and plastic yellow and orange dishes.

2 Petri dishes and covers
These dishes are great for growing crystals.

Liquid dropper
It's the perfect tool for cleaning out an egg…you'll see!

3 wooden sticks
Yum, yum. You'll grow your own sugar candy on these sticks.

1 chenille stem
Turn this item into a sparkling, crystal-covered star.

Pom-pom
You'll need this to make some erupting crystals!

Yarn
You'll be growing crystal stalactites (just like in caves) and fluffy snowflakes with the yarn in this kit.

Nylon string
You need this string to grow a very big crystal.

Magnifying glass
Check out the results of your experiments with this handy magnifier.

You should also get a notebook so you can make notes about your experiments.

CRYSTAL GROWING TIPS

Follow these simple tips to make the most of your crystal-growing experience.

DO:

- Follow the instructions carefully. Crystals won't grow if the conditions aren't just right.

- Make sure your measurements are correct.

- Write down times and dates in your experiment notebook. It's very easy to forget exactly when you started an experiment.

- Keep your experiments out of the sunlight, unless the directions say otherwise.

- Be patient. Some crystal-growing experiments take a long time. How long, exactly? The legend at the beginning of each experiment will give you a clue.

- Get a grownup to help you when an experiment says.

DON'T:

- Disturb your experiments while they are in progress. Doing this can affect the crystal-growing process.

- Give up too soon. The times given in this book are just guidelines. They may change depending on the room temperature, the humidity, the moon phase, the tides, the type of music you play.... Well, you get the idea. When it comes to growing crystals, you should always expect the unexpected!

LAST-MINUTE SAFETY STUFF

All of the materials in this book are safe to handle. But a good scientist always takes extra precautions. Here are a few guidelines you should follow:

- The materials in the experiments may sting your eyes. So wear safety glasses, if possible. If you do get anything into your peepers, rinse thoroughly with cold water.

- Wear rubber gloves when you touch washing soda, borax, laundry bluing, or window cleaner.

- Also wear rubber gloves when handling the Epsom salt crystals. These crystals are very sharp!

- Wash your hands after each experiment.

- No matter how hungry you may be, DO NOT EAT the experiments. One exception: The rock candy experiment on pages 32-33 is definitely munchable. But otherwise, no snacking.

- Get a grownup to help you with experiments that involve stoves. NO FOOLING. The instructions for these experiments tell you exactly when to get your grownup helper involved.

- And speaking of grownups…Keep your work area as clean as possible to avoid the wrath of Mom. (This is kind of a mental safety issue, but hey, it counts.)

That's it! You're prepped, you're pumped, you're ready for action.
So turn the page and let's get

GROWING!

EASY DOES IT

This section contains some super-simple crystal experiments that will get you started on your scientific journey. What makes them so easy? Well, you can set up each experiment within 5 minutes. You don't need any grownup help. And you'll get great results within one day or less. Interested? Then LET THE CRYSTAL-GROWING FUN BEGIN!

CRYSTAL TREE

Let's get this show started with a BANG! You're going to use the cardboard tree that came in your kit to grow a whole mess of fluffy crystals. Just follow the easy instructions, and then watch in amazement as your tree sprouts in every direction.

> You'll see changes in: 20 minutes
> Final results in: 8 hours

YOU NEED:

- Cardboard tree in your kit
- Orange plastic dish in your kit
- Liquid packet in your kit
- Scissors

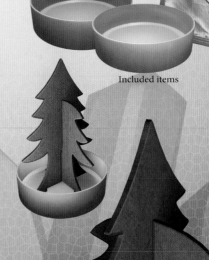

Included items

LET'S GET GROWING!

1. Punch out the two cardboard tree parts. Slide the big part onto the smaller part to build your tree.

2. Stand the tree in the orange plastic dish. Put the dish someplace where it won't be disturbed.

3. Use scissors to cut one corner off the liquid packet. Pick a corner, any corner. Carefully pour the liquid into the plastic dish.

4. Now sit back and watch. Right away, you'll see liquid creeping upward through the cardboard. Pretty soon the whole tree will be soaked…and now the real fun can begin! Tiny white hairs start to sprout from the edges of the tree. After a day or so, the whole tree will be covered with the little fuzzies.

WHAT'S GROWING ON?

A process called capillary action pulls the liquid from the dish up through the tree. The liquid carries a dissolved substance called potassium phosphate. This substance crystallizes when the liquid around it evaporates. (Phew! That's a whole lotta vocab words for one short blurb. It'll lighten up, we promise.)

ENCORE! ENCORE!

Did you love this experiment? Then you're in luck, because your kit comes with TWO crystal-growing gizmos! Just follow the instructions for the second tree, and wait to see what happens. (It's just as cool the second time around.)

GROW-NERS

Q: Why did the tree grow crystals instead of leaves?

A: It was tired of the same old thing. It wanted to branch out!

CRYSTAL'S TRIVIA CORNER

You know that slightly salty aftertaste you get when you guzzle sports drinks? Well, you can blame the stuff growing on your tree for that taste. Potassium phosphate is a salt, and yep, it's found in many athletic beverages.

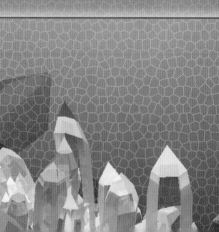

SPIKE'S SCIENCE SPOT

Let's talk a little bit more about capillary action. This phenomenon occurs because water is sticky. No, not to us—otherwise you'd feel like you had been dipped in honey whenever you took a shower! But other materials, including cardboard, stick to water like crazy. The attraction is strong enough to pull water from one place to another.

CRYSTAL ART

So you've done the big, fancy, pre-packaged experiment. And yep, it was cool. But now it's time to get down to basics. You're going to use plain old salt and water to create a colorful work of crystal art.

> You'll see changes in: 5 minutes
> Final results in: 15 minutes

LET'S GET GROWING!

1. Put 1 tablespoon (15 ml) of hot tap water and 1 teaspoon (5 ml) of salt into each disposable cup.

2. Stir each cup until the salt **dissolves**. This might take a while, so don't give up. Just keep stirring…and stirring…and stirring…Phew!

3. And now for some color! Drip a little food coloring into the cups. Use a different color for each cup. You have just made your very own crystal paint.

4. Use a paintbrush to create an original work of art on the black paper. Work fast—you should finish it up within a minute or so. Okay, so this painting will probably never make it into the Met, but don't worry about that right now.

5. Take your masterpiece outside. Set it in a sunny spot. Wait about 15 minutes for the paint to dry. When it does, you will see colorful, sparkly crystals stuck to the paper in exactly the shapes you painted!

YOU NEED:

- A sunny day
- 4 tablespoons (60 ml) hot tap water
- 4 teaspoons (20 ml) salt
- 4 disposable cups
- Stirring spoon
- Food coloring
- Paintbrush
- Black printer-type paper (not construction paper)

WHAT'S GROWING ON?

Water evaporates quickly under direct sunlight. Salt and food coloring do not. The water in your paint zips off the paper and into the air, leaving colorful salt crystals behind.

GROW-NERS

Q: What kind of eyes do gems have?

A: Crystallize!

CRYSTAL'S TRIVIA CORNER

A spice called sea salt forms when seawater evaporates. The leftover crystals are packaged and sold in grocery stores.

SPIKE'S SCIENCE SPOT

Why do you need a sunny day for this experiment? It's because the Sun speeds everything up. If you let your painting dry inside, the water would sit and sit, and it might soak into the paper along with the salt. Sure, the salt would still be there. But it wouldn't crystallize into that sparkly stuff.

ICE SPIKES

This experiment is super-easy to set up. But the results are really neat—and probably not what you would expect. Impress your pals with these spiky ice cubes that are cool in every possible way! (And just in case you were wondering: Yes, ice is a crystal.)

You'll see changes in: 2 hours

Final results in: 4 hours

YOU NEED:

- Ice cube tray
- Distilled water
- Freezer

LET'S GET GROWING!

1. Clean, rinse, and dry an ice cube tray. DON'T BE A SLACKER HERE. Do a good job. Use soap and a sponge, even.

2. Pour distilled water into the tray. For best results, fill up all of the little spaces.

3. Put the tray into the freezer. Let it sit for about four hours or until the water is completely frozen. Then check it out. Some of the ice cubes will have tall spikes growing out of them!

WHAT'S GROWING ON?

Water doesn't freeze in a flash. The process takes some time. First, the water gets cold and hardens near the edges of its container. Then, and only then, do the inner parts start to freeze. The longer the water stays in the freezer, the farther inward the ice grows. Here's where the spiky part comes in. Sometimes the icy edges of the cube squeeze the water in the middle. This water starts to bulge upward. After a while, it forms the spikes you saw in this experiment.

GROW-NERS

Q: What did the ice say to the angry water?

A: "You need to chill out, man!"

CRYSTAL'S TRIVIA CORNER

Tap water contains lots of dirt. (Yeah, and you drink the stuff!) This dirt stops ice spikes from growing. That's why this experiment needs distilled water, which is 100 percent dirt-free. That's also why you have to clean that ice cube tray before you begin the experiment.

SPIKE'S SCIENCE SPOT

Water turns into ice at 32 degrees Fahrenheit (0 degrees Celsius). But skating rinks keep things much colder than that. The ideal ice temp for figure skating is 22 degrees Fahrenheit (-5.5 degree Celsius). For hockey, it's even colder: 16 degrees Fahrenheit (-9 degrees Celsius) is the norm. BRRRR! No wonder the players wear so much padding!

FUZZY-WUZZY ROCKS

Rocks aren't like seeds. You can't stick a pebble into the ground and grow, say, a mountain. But the right rocks can grow crystals—and you're about to find out how to make it happen!

> You'll see changes in: 1 hour
> Final results in: 1 to 2 days

YOU NEED:

- One small piece of marble, limestone, or travertine (Check the garden section of your local home-improvement warehouse for loose pebbles.)
- Half of one of the Petri dishes in your kit
- Vinegar

LET'S GET GROWING!

1. Put the rock into the Petri dish.

2. Pour vinegar into the dish until it comes about halfway up the sides of the rock. The rock will start to fizz when the vinegar hits it. Oooooh, ahhhhh!

3. Now comes the waiting part. Leave your experiment alone until all of the vinegar has **evaporated**. (This may take a couple of days.) Peek into the dish every hour or two. You'll see more and more fluffy crystals sprouting from your rock!

WHAT'S GROWING ON?

The crystals that "fuzzify" your rock are a type of salt. They form when a mineral called calcium carbonate reacts with the vinegar in the dish. At first, the crystals are small. But they grow and grow as the vinegar evaporates.

GROW-NERS

Q: Why did the crystal dump her boyfriend?

A: He was taking her for granite!

CRYSTAL'S TRIVIA CORNER

Calcium carbonate is the active ingredient in antacids. You know, those round, chalky things you chew when your tummy feels icky. It's also found in vitamins.

SPIKE'S SCIENCE SPOT

So why does that rock fizz? It's because a chemical reaction occurs when calcium carbonate and vinegar meet. The reaction releases carbon dioxide gas, which forms bubbles before escaping into the air.

BOWL FULL OF CRYSTALS

This experiment is guaranteed to have you on pins and needles—of the crystal variety, of course! You'll fill a whole bowl with salty spikes in this easy experiment.

YOU NEED:

- ½ cup (120 ml) hot tap water
- ½ cup (120 ml) Epsom salt
- Small glass bowl
- Stirring spoon
- Fridge

> You'll see changes in: 1 hour
>
> Final results in: 6 hours

LET'S GET GROWING!

1. Put ½ cup (120 ml) of hot tap water and ½ cup (120 ml) of Epsom salt into a small glass bowl.

2. Stir until the Epsom salt **dissolves**. As always, be persistent. The process might take some elbow grease and a little time.

3. Put the bowl in the refrigerator. Now what do you do? Same as always—you wait, and you keep checking the bowl. In an hour or so, you'll see crystals forming in the water. A few hours after that, the entire bowl will be full of thin, transparent spikes. Hey, that's sharp!

WHAT'S GROWING ON?

The explanation for this one has to do with temperature, not evaporation. Hot water can hold a whole bunch of dissolved Epsom salt. Cold water, however, doesn't do the job quite as well. So when your water chills out in the fridge, the dissolved salt gets dumped out of the liquid solution. The tiny, rejected particles cling to each other. After a while, they form crystals that are big enough to see.

GROW-NERS

Q: Where do rocks and minerals go to have a good time?

A: To the crystal ball!

CRYSTAL'S TRIVIA CORNER

Epsom salt makes a great medicine! It can be used to treat heart conditions, asthma, migraines, and tetanus.

SPIKE'S SCIENCE SPOT

Did you know that crystals have habits? It's true! But we're not talking about nail biting or anything like that. In science-speak, the word "habit" refers to a crystal's size and shape. The crystals that grow from Epsom salt, for instance, have a needle-like habit.

Section II:

YOUR SKILLS ARE GROWING!

If you got through all the experiments in Section I, congratulations! Now you're ready to plunge a little deeper into the crystal scene. The activities in this section are a tad more complicated, and they take more time. Some even require grownup helpers. But hey, no sweat. It's crystal clear that your skills are growing, and you're up for the challenge!

SUPER-SIZED SALT

You know the salt that comes out of the shaker at dinnertime? The itsy-bitsy white sprinkles? Well, those are for wimps. In this experiment, you're going to make some really humongous salt cubes that are fit for a giant's table!

You'll see changes in: 1 day

Final results in: 1 week

YOU NEED:

- 1 cup (240 ml) hot tap water
- 3 tablespoons (45 ml) table salt
- Medium-size plastic food container
- Stirring spoon
- Fridge

LET'S GET GROWING!

1. Put 1 cup (240 ml) of hot tap water and 3 tablespoons (45 ml) of table salt into a medium-size plastic food container.

2. Stir until the salt **dissolves**. By now, you know the drill: It might take time. Keep going.

3. Pop the food container into the fridge. Try to find a spot where it won't be disturbed. Then let the growing begin! Within a week, your container will be full of giant—and perfectly square—salt crystals.

WHAT'S GROWING ON?

As the water evaporates, salt leaves the solution. Small particles join into larger ones and eventually into the giant chunks you see in your container. The chunks are square because salt has a square habit. For really impressive results, let this experiment continue for several weeks. Cubes up to ½ inch (1.2 cm) across may form by the time all of the water evaporates!

GROW-NERS

Q: Why didn't the salt hang out with the popular crowd?

A: He was much too square.

CRYSTAL'S TRIVIA CORNER

According to superstition, it's very unlucky to spill salt. You can solve the problem, though, by tossing a pinch of the spilled salt over your left shoulder. Just make sure no one is behind you at the time!

SPIKE'S SCIENCE SPOT

Salt just *loves* water. It bonds with moisture whenever it gets the chance. That's why people who live in damp places put rice inside salt shakers. The rice grains absorb water from the air before it can get to the salt. Without this help, the salt would quickly turn into a soggy, inedible lump.

GOOD GROWING, MR. LINCOLN!

For this experiment, we're going to use a coin that's part of the United States' currency. Try using different coins that are from other countries, too, and see what the results are!

> **You'll see changes in: 6 hours**
> **Final results in: 2 days**

YOU NEED:

- ¼ teaspoon (1.25 ml) salt
- 1 teaspoon (5 ml) vinegar
- Half of one of the Petri dishes in your kit
- Stirring spoon
- A penny

LET'S GET GROWING!

1. Put ¼ teaspoon (1.25 ml) of salt and 1 teaspoon (5 ml) of vinegar into one half of a Petri dish.

2. Stir until the salt **dissolves**. Be patient! It'll take several minutes of stirring to get the job done. Despite your best efforts, a few salt chunks may remain. This is okay.

3. Lay a penny in the Petri dish. Heads up, of course!

4. Put the dish someplace where it won't be disturbed. Then wait. (Have you realized yet that this is a standard part of crystal experiments?) You'll see green crystals growing on President Lincoln's face (and on the bottom and sides of the Petri dish, too) as the vinegar **evaporates**.

WHAT'S GROWING ON?

The salt can't stay **dissolved** when the vinegar **evaporates**. It starts to **crystallize** into square cubes on the bottom of the dish. It also forms fluffy fingers that creep up the dish's sides. At the same time, the salt picks up some copper from the penny. And pure copper is—you guessed it—GREEN!

GROW-NERS

Q: Why do pennies make good scientists?

A: They have lots of common cents!

CRYSTAL'S TRIVIA CORNER

There's a teeny, tiny statue of President Lincoln right in the middle of every penny's back side. What? You don't believe it? Use the magnifying glass that came in your kit to see for yourself!

SPIKE'S SCIENCE SPOT

You might have noticed that the vinegar/salt **solution** in this experiment doesn't just grow crystals. It cleans your penny, too. When salt and vinegar mix, they produce **ions** that snatch the grime right off the penny's surface. Luckily for your pocketbook, they don't harm the penny itself.

THAT'S EGGS-TRAORDINARY!

It takes a while to get through this whole *eggs*-periment. But the results are well worth the effort. You're going to turn regular eggshells into lumpy, bumpy crystal clumps. Are you *eggs*-cited? Yes? Then let's get cracking!

You'll see changes in: 5 days

Final results in: 2 weeks

CAUTION! Get a grownup to help you with this experiment.

YOU NEED:

- 3 eggs
- Resealable plastic container
- 1 cup (240 ml) vinegar
- 2 large disposable cups

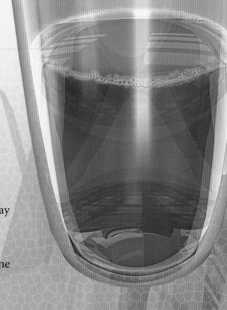

LET'S GET GROWING!

1. THE GROWNUP PART STARTS HERE. Crack the eggs. Dump the gooey insides into a resealable container. Save them for a Saturday-morning scramble. (You don't need them for this experiment.)

2. Thoroughly rinse the eggshells. Get all the goopy stuff out. THE GROWNUP PART ENDS HERE.

3. Pour 1 cup (240 ml) of vinegar into a large disposable cup. Crumble the eggshells and drop them into the vinegar. Fizz!!!

4. Let the vinegar/eggshell mixture sit for three days. Swirl the cup once a day to move the vinegar around.

5. After three days, pour the vinegar into another disposable cup. You're done with the other cup and the eggshells, so just throw them away.

6. Find a quiet place for the new cup. Check your experiment every couple of days. As the vinegar **evaporates**, you'll see white crystals forming on the sides of the cup. By the time the vinegar is completely gone, the cup will be full of bizarre crystal formations!

WHAT'S GROWING ON?

Eggshells are made mostly of calcium carbonate. (Hey, remember that stuff? It was in the crystal-growing rocks on pages 16-17, too.) The vinegar dissolves the calcium carbonate right out of the eggshells. You can't see it, but it's there in the liquid! Really! As the vinegar evaporates, the calcium carbonate crystals come together and form crystals.

GROW-NERS

Q: Why do eggs hate jokes?

A: They're afraid they might crack up!

CRYSTAL'S TRIVIA CORNER

How do you tell if an egg is hard-boiled or raw? Well, you can crack it, of course. But if you don't want to do that, just spin it. A hard-boiled egg spins quickly and easily. A raw egg, on the other hand, is slow and wobbly.

SPIKE'S SCIENCE SPOT

For a really cool and kinda gross trick, try growing BONE crystals. Let some old chicken or steak bones sit in vinegar for a few days. Then pour the vinegar into another cup and let it evaporate, just like you did with the *eggs*-periment on the previous page. I bet you can guess what will happen!

ERUPTING CRYSTALS

This experiment takes a day to set up. But once the legwork is done, things start moving very quickly. Spectacular washing soda crystals fill a bowl within minutes!

YOU NEED:

- ½ cup (120 ml) water
- 2 tablespoons (30 ml) washing soda (found in the laundry section of your grocery store)
- Pan
- Stirring spoon
- Small, heatproof glass bowl
- Fridge
- Pom-pom in your kit

You will not see ANY early changes.
Final results in: 1 day

CAUTION! Get a grownup to help you with this experiment.

LET'S GET GROWING!

1. Put ½ cup (120 ml) of water and 2 tablespoons (30 ml) of washing soda into a pan. Stir to mix everything together.

2. THE GROWNUP PART STARTS HERE. Put the pan on the stove. Heat the liquid until it just starts to simmer, then remove the pan from the heat.

3. Pour the hot liquid into the glass bowl. Then put the bowl into the fridge. THE GROWNUP PART ENDS HERE.

4. Let the mixture sit for one whole day. We're talking 24 hours here. DON'T DISTURB THE EXPERIMENT.

5. After the day has passed, drop the pom-pom into the mixture. Then sit back and watch the show. Within 15 minutes, a large crystal will erupt below the pom-pom!

WHAT'S GROWING ON?

Before that pom-pom arrives, the washing soda isn't quite ready to crystallize. But afterward, everything changes. The pom-pom sheds tiny particles that make perfect crystal-growing platforms. The washing soda clings to these particles as it leaps willy-nilly out of the solution. It forms huge spikes before you can say, "Holy crystallization, Batman!"

GROW-NERS

Q: Why are chemists so good at solving problems?

A: They're always surrounded by solutions!

CRYSTAL'S TRIVIA CORNER

The temperature inside the average fridge is about 43 degrees Fahrenheit (6 degrees Celsius).

SPIKE'S SCIENCE SPOT

Why do you need to refrigerate the washing-soda solution? It's because your chilly fridge gets the mixture good and ready to crystallize. By the time 24 hours have passed, that washing soda is just dying to come out of the solution. The pom-pom gives it exactly the push it needs.

TWINKLE, TWINKLE, CRYSTAL STAR

This experiment wants to be the star of the show! It certainly has the right shape for it—and the talent, too. You're going to be star-struck for sure when you see these stellar results!

You'll see changes in: 2 hours

Final results in: 8 hours

CAUTION! Get a grownup to help you with this experiment.

YOU NEED:

- Chenille stem in your kit
- Thread
- Pencil
- See-through, heatproof glass container
- 2 cups (480 ml) water
- ½ cup (120 ml) borax (found in the laundry section of your grocery store)
- Pan
- Stirring spoon
- Plate
- Fridge

LET'S GET GROWING!

1. Bend the chenille stem into the shape of a star. It's a little tricky to get the proportions right, but hey, it doesn't have to be PERFECT! When you're done, twist the loose ends of the chenille stem to hold everything together.

2. Tie a piece of thread to the star. Tie the other end of the thread to a pencil. NOW FOR THE DROP TEST. Lower the star into your glass container. Set the pencil across the opening. The star should not touch the bottom of your glass container. If it does, it's time to adjust the string! RETEST until the thread is the right length.

3. Take the star out of the container when you're done testing.

4. Here we go with the main event! Put 2 cups (480 ml) of water and ½ cup (120 ml) of borax into a pan. Stir to mix everything together.

5. THE GROWNUP PART STARTS HERE. Put the pan on the stove. Heat the liquid until it just starts to simmer, then remove the pan from the heat.

6. Pour the hot liquid into the glass container.

7. Dunk the star in the liquid. Then set the star on a plate to dry. You can't see it, but teeny-weeny crystals are forming on the star at this very moment.

8. After about 15 minutes, lower the star into the liquid so the pencil lies across the jar's opening. Stick everything into the fridge. THE GROWNUP PART ENDS HERE.

9. Check on your experiment every hour or so. After about two hours, you will see crystals forming on your star. After about eight hours, the star will be caked with glittering chunks. Twinkle, twinkle!

What's Growing On?

By heating the water/borax mixture, you make it possible for lots and lots of borax to dissolve. The borax is perfectly happy when the mixture is hot. But when things cool down, the borax can't stay dissolved. It leaves the solution and forms crystals—right on your dangling star.

Grow-ners

Q: Why do stars always win games?

A: They start out with five extra points!

Crystal's Trivia Corner

In the late 1800s, mule teams pulled borax-filled wagons from mines to trains. That's why some borax products show pictures of donkeys. Hee-Haw!

Spike's Science Spot

Scientists have a word for little crystals (like the ones from Step 7 of this experiment) that are used to grow bigger ones. They call them seed crystals. These crystals are not really seeds. But they do give smaller particles a place to attach themselves. This makes it easier for crystallization to take place.

EAT-'EM-UP CRYSTAL CRUNCHIES

Are all these experiments making you hungry? Good, because it's snack time! You're about to make some sugary crystals that are tasty as well as beautiful.

You'll see changes in: 15 minutes
Final results in: 1 day

CAUTION!
Get a grownup to help you with this experiment.

YOU NEED:

- 1 cup (240 ml) water
- 2½ cups (600 ml) sugar
- Pan
- Stirring spoon
- See-through, heatproof glass container
- Wooden stick in your kit
- Plate
- Scissors
- Disposable plastic lid (like the snap-on kind from margarine tubs)

LET'S GET GROWING!

1. Put 1 cup (240 ml) of water and 2½ cups (600 ml) of sugar into a pan. Stir to mix everything together.

2. THE GROWNUP PART STARTS HERE. Put the pan on the stove and bring the liquid to a gentle simmer. Let it simmer for about 30 minutes. Stir the liquid every now and then.

3. Pour the hot liquid into a glass container. BE CAREFUL.

4. Dip a wooden stick from your kit into the liquid. Remove it and set it on a plate to dry. You know what's up: You're forming **seed crystals**.

5. When the stick is dry, use scissors to poke a small hole in the middle of the plastic lid. Push the clean end of the stick through the hole.

6. Set the lid on top of the glass container so the stick hangs down into the hot, sugary liquid. Phew. The dangerous part is over! THE GROWNUP PART ENDS HERE.

7. Watch the container carefully. Within 15 minutes, you will see tiny crystals growing on the stick. A day later, the entire stick will be covered with rocklike chunks. Pull the stick out of the liquid and let it dry, then take a big bite. Delicious!

Use the extra sticks in your kit to repeat the experiment. Treats all around!

WHAT'S GROWING ON?

The sugar in your solution wants to crystallize—and the teensy crystals on your wooden stick give the dissolved sugar the perfect foothold. Billions and billions of little sugar particles attach themselves to the stick to form a crystal-rrific treat!

GROW-NERS

Q: What did the sugar crystals name their band?

A: Rock Candy, of course!

CRYSTAL'S TRIVIA CORNER

Candy makers say rock candy syrup is at the "hard-ball" stage. This means that a blob of the syrup will form a hard ball if it is dropped into cold water.

SPIKE'S SCIENCE SPOT

When you do this experiment, you'll have a delicious stickload of rock candy within a day. But the fun doesn't stop there! Set the jar in a quiet place and watch as crystals continue to form. The whole jar will be rocking out after a week or so!

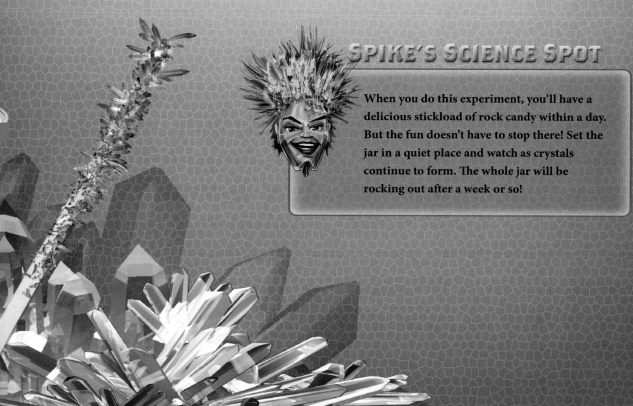

Section III:

SIMPLY SPECTACULAR!

You're about to enter the home stretch of your race for crystal knowledge. This section features bigger, better experiments that are just right for an expert like yourself! These activities are a little harder to set up than the simple stuff you tried earlier. But they produce seriously spectacular results. Get ready to indulge yourself in some truly fantastic crystal fun!

CRYSTAL SCULPTURE

This experiment is a true stunner, and it's not even very hard to set up. Prepare to go crystal crazy!

> You'll see changes in: 1 hour
> Final results in: 1½ days

CAUTION!
Get a grownup to help you with this experiment.

LET'S GET GROWING!

1. Put 1 teaspoon (5 ml) of hot tap water and 1 teaspoon (5 ml) of Epsom salt into half of a Petri dish. Stir to mix everything together.

2. Put the Petri dish into the fridge. Let it sit until the **solution** has completely **crystallized**. This will probably take about 24 hours.

3. Put ½ cup (120 ml) of hot tap water and ½ cup (120 ml) of Epsom salt into a small glass bowl. Stir to mix everything together.

4. Now let's combine everything! Use duct tape to stick a quarter to the bottom of the Petri dish. You'll see why in a moment.

5. Gently lower the Petri dish into the bowl. The quarter helps the dish to sink. (See? There WAS a good reason!)

6. Put everything into the fridge. Then wait six to eight hours. After this period, you'll see a mass of crystals sprouting from the Petri dish.

7. Use a fork, if necessary, to fish the Petri dish out of the bowl. Set the dish on a paper towel. While it's drying, gasp in amazement at the lovely crystal sculpture you have created!

YOU NEED:

- 1 teaspoon (5 ml) plus ½ cup (120 ml) hot tap water
- 1 teaspoon (5 ml) plus ½ cup (120 ml) Epsom salt
- Half of one of the Petri dishes in your kit
- Stirring spoon
- Fridge
- Small glass bowl
- Duct tape
- A quarter or other heavy coin
- Fork
- Paper towel

WHAT'S GROWING ON?

The Epsom salt crystals in the Petri dish act as seed crystals. The crystal pile grows and grows as it attracts more particles from the solution in the bowl.

GROW-NERS

Q: Why did the solution have a hard time getting to sleep?

A: It was all stirred up!

CRYSTAL'S TRIVIA CORNER

Petri dishes are named after Julius Richard Petri, a German scientist. Petri invented his now-famous dish in 1877, to the delight of researchers everywhere.

SPIKE'S SCIENCE SPOT

If you put Epsom salt into your bathtub, your skin won't get so wrinkly. Why? Your skin prunes up ONLY when it absorbs water. Skin can absorb a lot more pure water than salty water. So by salting your surroundings, you reduce the prune factor big time.

EGG GEODE

A geode is a hollow rock that contains crystals. Okay, so an egg isn't a rock, but you can turn it into a geode-like crystal container. Check it out in this sp-*egg*-tacular *egg*-speriment! You'll need a lot of grownup help for this one, but it's worth it.

> You will not see ANY early changes.
> Final results in: 2 days

CAUTION!
Get a grownup to help you with this experiment.

YOU NEED:

- Thumbtack
- 1 egg
- Liquid dropper in your kit
- Food container
- ½ cup (120 ml) water
- 2 tablespoons (30 ml) borax
- Pan
- Stirring spoon
- Egg tray
- Fridge

LET'S GET GROWING!

1. THE GROWNUP PART STARTS HERE. Use a thumbtack to poke a small hole in the egg's narrower point. You should just be able to fit the tip of the liquid dropper into the hole.

2. Hold the egg over a food container with the hole facing downward. Poke the liquid dropper into the hole. Squeeze the dropper to force air into the egg, then pull the dropper out. Raw egg goo will come streaming out of the egg. Repeat this process until the egg is empty. (Why the food container? It's to help you save the egg goo. Have yourself a nice omelet for breakfast.)

3. Use the dropper to squirt water into the egg. SHAKE, SHAKE, SHAKE to clean the egg. Then turn the egg upside down over a sink. Use the dropper as you did in Step 2 to get the water out of the egg.

4. Put ½ cup (120 ml) of water and 2 tablespoons (30 ml) of borax into a pan. Stir to mix everything together.

5. Put the pan on the stove. Heat the liquid until it just starts to simmer, then remove the pan from the heat. Let the pan sit for about 15 minutes. (This will give the liquid some time to cool down.)

6. Put your empty eggshell in an egg tray or anything else that will keep it standing upright. The hole should be on top.

7. Use the liquid dropper to fill the egg with the borax mixture. ALL THE WAY TO THE TOP, NOW. Then put the egg into the fridge. THE GROWNUP PART ENDS HERE

8. Leave the egg alone for two days. That's 48 entire hours. When the time is up, carefully crack the egg open. The inner cavity is coated with shiny crystals!

WHAT'S GROWING ON?

The borax can't stay dissolved when the water cools. It starts to crystallize on every available surface—which, in this case, is the inside of an eggshell.

GROW-NERS

Q: Why did the geode go to the dentist?

A: Because it had a cavity!

CRYSTAL'S TRIVIA CORNER

Your geode is, well, egg-sized. But real geodes can be much larger than this. The biggest geode ever found was 33 feet (10 m) long, 16½ feet (5 m) high, and 10 feet (3 m) wide. That's as big as a school bus!

SPIKE'S SCIENCE SPOT

Here's how to pick up liquid with the dropper, folks. First, squeeze the bulb on the end of the dropper. Next, plunge the dropper's tip into some liquid and release the bulb. Finally, poke the dropper's tip wherever you want the liquid to go. Squeeze again to squirt the liquid out of the dropper. Ta-da!

WILD AND WOOLLY CRYSTAL GARDEN

This is a classic crystal experiment—and with good reason. It's cool! Follow the steps below to create a snowy crystal landscape that is sure to knock your socks off.

> **You'll see changes in: 3 hours**
> **Final results in: 3 days**

CAUTION!
Get a grownup to help you with this experiment.

LET'S GET GROWING!

1. Smear shortening all over the insides of a plastic food container. This will stop crystals from creeping up the sides of the container.

2. Break up three or four charcoal briquets. Pick out a bunch of large chunks and set them in the food container.

3. THE GROWNUP PART STARTS HERE. Put ¼ cup (60 ml) each of warm tap water, liquid laundry bluing, window cleaner, and salt into a large disposable cup. Stir the mixture until all of the salt **dissolves**.

4. Pour the liquid right onto those briquets. Really douse them. Pour until the bottom two-thirds of each briquet are submerged or until you run out of liquid, whichever comes first. THE GROWNUP PART ENDS HERE.

5. Drip food coloring onto the damp briquets. Use as many colors as you like.

6. Sprinkle salt all over the briquets.

7. Put your experiment in a quiet place. Check it once every couple of hours. Soon you will see hairy little growths sprouting from the briquets. After a few days, the entire container will be blanketed with colorful crystals!

YOU NEED:

- Cooking shortening
- Sandwich-size plastic food container
- 3 or 4 charcoal briquets
- ¼ cup (60 ml) warm tap water
- ¼ cup (60 ml) liquid laundry bluing (available in grocery stores)
- ¼ cup (60 ml) window cleaner with ammonia
- ¼ cup (60 ml) plus a few extra pinches of salt
- Large disposable cup
- Stirring spoon
- Food coloring

WHAT'S GROWING ON?

The laundry bluing contains teeny-weeny metallic particles. As the water in the solution evaporates, these particles act like seed crystals. In other words, they give the salt someplace to grow. The charcoal briquets suck up the bluing and the salt and eject them upward as fluffy white crystals. As for the window cleaner, it just speeds up the rate of evaporation so you get results more quickly. Yes, we're all about instant gratification here.

GROW-NERS

Q: What did the charcoal say when it got to know the salt?

A: "I think you're growing on me!"

CRYSTAL'S TRIVIA CORNER

Laundry bluing is sometimes used to mark skiways. Officials mix bluing with water, then spray it onto the snow. This process creates shockingly bright lines that are easy for skiers to see. Blue lips, blue lines…it's all part of that winter sports experience!

SPIKE'S SCIENCE SPOT

This experiment will keep going as long as you want it to. Just mix up new batches of growing solution and pour some into your tray whenever the liquid level gets low. Then watch as the crystal mess increases. Crystal garden? Ha! I laugh at your puny garden. Crystal farm is more like it!

JUST HANGING AROUND

Are you ready to make a big mess? Yes? Good, because this experiment is pretty sloppy. But the results are really neat!

> **You'll see changes in: 2 hours**
> **Final results in: 2 days**

CAUTION!
Get a grownup to help you with this experiment.

YOU NEED:

- Half of the yarn in your kit (cut the long strand in half)
- 2 large paper clips
- 2 cups (480 ml) water
- ½ cup (120 ml) washing soda
- Pan
- Stirring spoon
- 2 heatproof containers (coffee mugs work great)
- Cookie tray or other large baking sheet with raised edges

LET'S GET GROWING!

1. Tie a large paper clip to each end of the yarn. The paper clips weight the yarn down and keep it from flopping around or floating.

2. Put 2 cups (480 ml) of water and ½ cup (120 ml) of washing soda into a pan. Stir to mix everything together.

3. THE GROWNUP PART STARTS HERE. Put the pan on the stove. Heat the liquid until it just starts to simmer, then remove the pan from the heat. Let the pan sit for about 15 minutes. (This will give the liquid some time to cool down.)

4. Set two heatproof containers on a baking sheet. Pour half of the hot liquid into each container.

5. Dunk the yarn into one cup. Get it totally wet. Then arrange the yarn so it dangles between the containers with one end in each container, as shown. Move the cups toward or away from each other until the middle part of the yarn droops, as shown. Almost immediately, liquid will start dripping from the yarn's lowest point. THE GROWNUP PART ENDS HERE.

6. Let everything DRIP, DRIP, DRIP. After a couple of hours, you will notice that the yarn is coated with something vaguely **crystalline**. A big lump will start to grow on the droopy part of the yarn. Within two days, the lump will ooze downward to form a crystal stalactite that looks just like the ones in caves. Bring on the bats!

WHAT'S GROWING ON?

Capillary action (remember that?) sucks the liquid into the yarn. The liquid flows right through the yarn and falls out at the lowest point. As it falls, however, it leaves little bits of washing soda behind. These little bits build up over time. Eventually they join to form a solid crystal column.

GROW-NERS

Q: How did the stalactite and the stalagmite end their quarrel?

A: They agreed to meet each other halfway!

CRYSTAL'S TRIVIA CORNER

In a cave, formations that hang from the ceiling are called stalactites. The ones that that poke up from the floor are called stalagmites. To remember which is which, remind yourself that stalactites have to stick *tite* to keep from falling!

SPIKE'S SCIENCE SPOT

For a faster growing experience, use a ½-inch by 12-inch (1.2-cm by 30-cm) towel strip instead of yarn. Why? A towel strip is much thicker than the yarn, so it'll suck up that washing soda in no time flat.

SNOWFLAKES ON A STRING

Hey, is it snowing in here? This experiment is a lot like the last one. But the materials and, most importantly, the results are different. Try it and see! (Oh, and here's some great news: You don't need a grownup for this one.)

> **You'll see changes in: 2 hours**
> **Final results in: 4 days**

YOU NEED:

- Half of the yarn in your kit
- 2 large paper clips
- 2 cups (480 ml) hot tap water
- ⅓ cup (80 ml) baking soda
- Bowl
- Stirring spoon
- 2 glasses
- Cookie tray or other large baking sheet with raised edges

LET'S GET GROWING!

1. Tie a large paper clip to each end of the yarn. You already know why from the last experiment.

2. Put 2 cups (480 ml) of hot tap water and ⅓ cup (80 ml) of baking soda into a bowl. Stir to mix everything together. This is going to take some effort, because it takes baking soda a while to **dissolve**. Hop to it!

3. Set two glasses on a baking sheet. Pour half of the liquid into each container.

4. Dunk the yarn into one cup to get it wet. Then arrange the yarn as you did in the last experiment. Get a slow drip going.

5. Check your experiment every now and then to make sure it's still drippy. After about two hours, white hairy things will start growing out of the yarn. The hairs will grow and grow over the next few days until they look a little bit like snowflakes. But not icicles. You'll never get a stalactite like the one you made in the last experiment.

WHAT'S GROWING ON?

Baking soda crystallizes differently than washing soda. Instead of coating the yarn, it grows outward in all directions. It's so busy growing on the yarn, in fact, that it can't be bothered to travel all the way to the stalactite-forming spot. Hey, different material, different priorities.

GROW-NERS

Q: What type of soda goes best with homemade cookies?

A: Baking soda!

CRYSTAL'S TRIVIA CORNER

Baking soda is one of the handiest products on the market. Besides growing snowflakes, it's used in baking, odor removal, all-purpose cleaning, hair care, and even fire control. Yep, the stuff is found inside some fire extinguishers.

SPIKE'S SCIENCE SPOT

Real snowflakes are crystals, too—and no two snowflakes are exactly alike. See for yourself! On a snowy day, let some flakes land on a piece of black paper. Carry the paper to a windless spot. Then examine the flakes with your magnifying glass. How many different shapes can you find?

SUPER-SIZED SPARKLER

And now for the grand finale of our book. It's big…it's bold…it's a super-sized crystal you can grow yourself! This experiment takes a long time, but don't let that discourage you. Remember, good things come to those who wait.

> You'll see changes in: 2 hours
> Final results in: 3 to 4 weeks

LET'S GET GROWING!

1. Put 2 tablespoons (30 ml) of hot tap water and 1 teaspoon (5 ml) of alum into a disposable cup. Stir to mix everything together.

2. And now for a short break in our experiment. Set the cup aside and wait until all of the water **evaporates**. This may take a few days. When the cup is bone-dry, the bottom will be coated with alum crystals.

3. Time to spring back into action! Break a good-sized chunk off the crystal sheet. Tie one end of the plastic string from your kit around the chunk. Tie the other end of the string to a pencil.

4. Carefully lower the crystal into the baby food jar. Adjust the length of the string until the crystal hangs JUST BELOW THE CENTER of the jar when the pencil rests across the top. When everything looks perfect, set the pencil and the chunk aside.

5. Now for the crystal-growing **solution**! Put ½ cup (120 ml) of hot tap water and 2 tablespoons (30 ml) of alum into a bowl. Stir to mix everything together.

6. Pour the mixture into the baby food jar. Then gently lower the crystal chunk into the liquid. Rest the pencil across the jar's mouth. Set everything in a quiet place where it won't be disturbed for weeks (and weeks, and weeks). Check the experiment every now and then to see how your crystal is doing.

YOU NEED:

- 2 tablespoons (30 ml) plus ½ cup (120 ml) hot tap water
- 1 teaspoon (5 ml) plus 2 tablespoons (30 ml) alum (found in the spice section of some grocery stores)
- Disposable cup
- Stirring spoon
- Nylon string in your kit
- Pencil
- Clean, dry baby food jar or another small, see-through container of about the same size
- Bowl

WHAT'S GROWING ON?

That crystal chunk you tied to the string? Yes, that's a big fat seed crystal. It acts like a gathering place for the alum particles in your solution. They all rush inward to join the party. The longer you wait, the bigger your crystal will grow!

GROW-NERS

Q: What kind of crystals do you find at high-school reunions?

A: Alums!

CRYSTAL'S TRIVIA CORNER

This isn't really trivia. It's more like a note of encouragement. You need to know that alum can be hard to find. But this mission is NOT impossible. Go to all the different grocery stores in your area, if necessary. One of them is bound to have the stuff.

SPIKE'S SCIENCE SPOT

For extra-large results, mix up another batch of alum solution as in Step 5 of this experiment. Add some of the new solution to your jar whenever the liquid level drops. The growth process will continue until your patience runs out!

GLOSSARY

Atom: The smallest possible particle of a chemical element.

Capillary action: A process that occurs when liquid is attracted to certain materials. The attraction moves the liquid from one place to another.

Chemical reaction: A chemical change that happens when two or more substances come into contact.

Crystal: A solid substance in which the atoms and molecules form repeating patterns.

Crystalline: Looking like a crystal or made of crystals.

Crystallize: To change into a crystal form.

Dissolve: To pass into a solution.

Evaporate: To change from a solid or gas into a vapor form.

Geode: A rock that contains a crystal-filled cavity.

Habit: The crystal shape and growth method of a certain material.

Ion: Any atom or group of atoms that has an unequal number of protons and electrons.

Molecule: A neutral group of two or more atoms.

React: See chemical reaction.

Seed crystal: A crystal that acts as a growing surface for more crystals.

Solution: A liquid that contains a dissolved solid.